Pictures in Clouds

What do you see in a cloud?

Sue Carson

Pictures in Clouds
Copyright © 2022 by Sue Carson

All rights reserved. No part of this publication may be reproduced, distributed, or transmitted in any form or by any means, including photocopying, recording, or other electronic or mechanical methods, without the prior written permission of the author, except in the case of brief quotations embodied in critical reviews and certain other non-commercial uses permitted by copyright law.

Tellwell Talent
www.tellwell.ca

ISBN
978-0-2288-5026-7 (Paperback)

This Book is dedicated to my Saltlings:

Daniel, Benjamin & Colin
And their
Na Na, my Mom, Isabel

"Daniel, Daniel, look up at the sky! I see a dinosaur way up high!

Do you see it, Dan?"

"Actually, Benjamin, do you know what I see in the sky?

Look where I am pointing, Ben. I see lots of long **Cirrus Clouds**! Cirrus Clouds look like they have been s-t-r-e-t-c-h-e-d into long strands. They are made of up of thin ice crystals, and it usually means we are going to have a nice weather day!"

"Daniel, Daniel, look up at the sky! I see a huge whale way up high!

Do you see it, Dan?"

"Actually, Benjamin, do you know what I see in the sky?

I see a sky that is starting to form the most amazing **Stratus Clouds**! Look under the cloud that looks like a Turtle! See the thick cloud forming? That is Stratus Cloud. Soon it will form a thick blanket across the sky and then we can expect rain. Stratus Clouds form when warmer, wet air blows in. Ben, the whales in the oceans would see lots of Stratus Clouds because fog is a Stratus Cloud! Fog is a cloud that forms close to the ground or water."

"Daniel, Daniel, look up at the sky! I see a dragon way up high!

Do you see it, Dan?"

"Actually, Benjamin, do you know what I see in the sky?

I see the most beautiful puffy pile of **Cumulus Clouds**! The word Cumulus means 'pile'. That's how you remember cumulus clouds Ben. They pile up! When they are white and fluffy like today, it usually means it will remain a nice day, but when they turn grey it could mean that it is going to rain! Do you see anything else hiding in those Cumulus Clouds, Ben?"

"Colin said he saw a duck in the clouds, I can't see it Dan, can you?"

"Benjamin, Benjamin, look up at the sky! I see a steam train way up high!

Do you see it, Ben?"

"Actually, Dan, do you know what **I** see in the sky?

I see what a meteorologist would call a perfect example of **Nimbus Clouds**! That steam you see is heavy rain falling from the Nimbus Cloud and those sparks you see are lightning flashes! Nimbus Clouds always have rain or snow falling from them! Today it's rain with lightning! Let's listen for the boom of thunder that comes after the lightning flash."

"You are right Ben. I see those Nimbus Clouds!"
"You are right too, Dan, because now I can clearly see that steam train with sparks coming from the wheels!

"Daniel, Benjamin look up at the sky because I see Nimbus-Birds way up high!
Do you see them?

An Eye to the Sky

Take some time, look at the sky,
Imagine pictures way up high.
What's in the clouds floating by,
A rabbit or a butterfly?

As you wonder how and why,
Let Science help identify.
How do clouds form in the sky?
What makes them shift and modify?

Cirrus Clouds, thin wisps so high,
S t r e t c h out across the wide blue sky.
Look way up and if you try,
A dinosaur might catch your eye!

Stratus Clouds blanket nearby
In hanging fog what can you spy?
Whales swim through and come say "hi",
Then slap their tails and wave goodbye.

Cumulus Clouds, pile so high-
If not too dark, it will stay dry.
Dragons soar and roar and sigh-
Spew smoke and fire as they cry.

Nimbus Clouds in good supply,
Rain, snow, or hail you can't deny.
Steam Engines with sparks fly by,
Lightning flashes...Thunder...Oh my!

What do YOU see way up high?
So much to see and wonder why!

Epilogue

There is something that children and adults in every corner of this world do.

We look up at the sky. Sometimes we see clouds. To some of us those clouds can be turned into pictures that shift and change with wind and time. For others, they spark curiosity about the science of those clouds and for still others it is the beauty and the mystery that keep us looking up to our skies.

We can learn from each other when we appreciate things differently and we can all work together to protect our beautiful earth and the skies that surround us all.

Next time you go outside and have some time, lie on your back and look up.

What do you see way up high?

What do you see in the sky?

Special thanks to Editors:

My husband, Phil
&
Fun-friend, Clare
(Poet extraordinaire)

www.ingramcontent.com/pod-product-compliance
Lightning Source LLC
LaVergne TN
LVHW071656060526
838200LV00030B/475